How To Spy On Your Neighbor

Your Survival Guide for the

United States of Russia

Vicky Kuperman and Isabella Patrick

No part of the contents of this book relate to any real person or persons, living or dead.

ISBN-13: 978-0692034316
ISBN-10: 0692034315

This book is dedicated to the resistance.

Table of Contents

Spasiba

This book was written under the surveillance of Brandi Bowles-kaya, who is the best agent and editor in the world. She gets us. She really gets us!

Angelin Borsics-ova, who was the first person who heard the idea (thank god she laughed) and remains one of its biggest champions.

Rakesh Satyal-ivov, who had the brilliant mind to send the project to Brandi. The rest is re-written Russian history!

Max Cohen-shnikov, a survivor of a Russian regime in his own home.

Jay Patrick-ovich, who is practically a Russian.

Leo and Laela: Spasibs:)

Aalap Patel-ov for his amazing Crimea joke.

Jarrod Taylor-ovsky for being brilliant like a Russian.

Thank you to our parents for bringing us to this country where we get good dental work and for instilling the fear and paranoia in us that was necessary to write this book.

Thank you to all the random cafes and restaurants in New York City we sat in while we wrote this book, and who didn't kick us out even though we brought our own food. It was hard to think over our cacophonous laughter. Sorry to the other patrons (except that one guy on his Bluetooth - you know who you are).

Introduction

Privet! In recent years, there's been a lot of bad P.R. about Russia and the Soviet Union.

Spoiler: It was all true!

This handy survival guide will teach you everything you need to know about surviving our United States of Russia new world order. We hope you have a great memory because taking notes is a no-no. The government could find them and lock you up. If that happens though, we've got you covered (see chapter three for prison camp survival etiquette).

We'd tell you to sit back and relax while we put the "rad" back in comrade, but then you'll be vulnerable. From this day forward you must have eyes in the back of your head. You never know who's watching, listening, taking notes, videotaping you, wiretapping you or laughing at you. Your life as you know it is over!

P.S. Burn after reading. It's socially acceptable to burn books now! How else are you going to stay warm?

Chapter 1: Surviving the apocalypse in four-inch heels

As a citizen of the United States of Russia you'll need to redefine your basic survival skills. Everything you're used to is about to change, from the clothes you wear to the people you trust (don't trust anyone).

DRESS TO IMPRESS (THE COPS)

Women:

Days in Russia are long, dark and frigid. For optimal energy, start your day off on the right foot…in four-inch stiletto heels. Keep them by your bed for easy slip-on access. Then throw on a leopard print dress, a fur scarf, your 14-carat diamond necklace, and some red lipstick. This opulent ensemble will help you pass for Russian. Even better, if you get arrested on suspicious behavior, you'll have enough to bribe your way into a better jail cell.

Be sure to dress like a high-class prostitute on your way to the grocery store or the dry cleaner. You never know who you'll run into (like a potential client or constable). Dress like a supermodel even if you're just at home answering your phone or curing herring. You never know what neighbors are spying on you. Even when you're "dressed down" in sweatpants you'll still be in full make-up, a fur vest, carrying an enormous (stolen) Louis Vuitton duffel, and high heel high-top Coach sneakers.

If you're reporting your neighbor to the authorities, three words: always wear makeup. The police will only take you seriously if you flirt with them and look like you're on your way to the Miss Universe Pageant.

Carry a nice wad of cash tucked into your underwear, so if you're crotch-frisked it will serve as a silent "nod" to the police. Allow them to retrieve the crotch cash, and then you will be free to go about the rest of your day. Simple, right? You'll get used to it.

Men:

Wear a black, velour ADIDAS tracksuit with a lot of hidden interior pockets (silent Velcro or magnetic closures are best). They're great for carrying wads of cash, hiding wiretaps, and concealing pocket knives. You will need ample storage to carry all of your extra multi-national passports - just in case. Keep your ADIDAS tracksuit fresh by wearing a clean wife-beater. It's ok, we can call it that now (see chapter four). You can only dream of one day being able to afford a $3,000 tracksuit for the gym, like Putin. This is one of many ways you'll strive to emulate and honor him.

You won't need to put on your Bluetooth earpiece in the morning, because you've slept in it! The Bluetooth is a key element of leading a double life. This earpiece is great for receiving information without anyone noticing. It may look like you're sleeping, but you're really getting intel from your cousin about who in your network has been arrested today and which streets to avoid. It would also be helpful to learn some ventriloquism.

Women and men:

Fur is key for almost every outfit. Conveniently, fur is getting cheaper now that there are no hunting laws and you can shoot for your own hats and coats! Save the meat, 'cause you'll need it for dinner. A camping trip to the state park used to mean a family vacation. Now it means shopping for clothes and groceries.

No child should be left behind, so put that rifle in your kids' hands and make them earn their keep. This way, they can perfect their aim for when a grizzly bear wanders into their classroom during geography.

If you're already part of the NRA, all of this should be a seamless transition. For everyone else: get on board or starve. And don't reveal that you're not an existing NRA member. Just get a gun and put that sticker on your window.

Transgender people:

You'll be wearing striped prison uniforms.

RATIONS

To survive an autocratic regime, proper nourishment is key. If you eat too much, your aunt will pull you aside and tell you you're fat. Just kidding! She'll do it in front of everyone. If you don't eat enough, your mother's best friend will pull you aside and ask why you're so skinny. Either way, your eating habits will be perceived as suspicious, so have your defense mechanisms at-hand (cash bribes and handkerchiefs for hiding or spitting out food).

Due to impending low food supply, you will have to learn how to grow your own potatoes in your backyard, or community garden. If your potato crop does well you can make vodka in your bathtub! Vodka is now an acceptable form of currency, and also used as an anesthetic. Keep small vials of it stashed in your velour tracksuit or hidden in your cleavage. The potato is great for many purposes: food, vodka, weapon, stamp, paper-weight and soccer ball.

If you're having people over for dinner, all the food has to be out and ready to serve when they arrive. This is mostly so that if your neighbor happens to be reporting you at that moment (highly, HIGHLY likely) and the police stop by, they won't pick up on what's really happening, even if everyone's secretly gathered to read banned literature like the NY Times, listening to

banned music like The Beatles or watching
bootleg footage of CNN or that clip of Obama
singing Al Green.

To keep the ruse going, take everything out of
the refrigerator and place it randomly on the
table. Sardines next to butter; bread next to
potatoes; borscht next to fruit; vodka next to the
baby's milk. Russian dinner parties have no rules.
Relish in it. Oh, and speaking of relish, it makes
for a great centerpiece for the dessert tray. Don't
forget to sprinkle everything with chopped dill.
In fact, large bunches of dill are a great place to
conceal your most precious jewels and reverse
wire taps. Nobody will question why you have
so much dill. There can never be enough dill!

Say goodbye to your huge American kitchen.
Times are tough and you need all the square
footage to house distant family members and
stockpile nonperishable goods. You will soon be
cooking on a hot-plate atop a dresser in a closet
where you may have an uncle sleeping on a cot
beneath you. From here he listens to the
neighbor's conversations through the vent. This
is actually extremely handy because he's also
within ear-shot of street noise and has become a
real master at identifying a policeman's footsteps.
If food drops out of your hand, he will catch it
with his mouth. This is his only daily food ration.
The uncle, the kitchen, the vent and the food
scraps all might seem random, but they're a

perfected and self-sustaining eco-system. Accept it, maneuver it, and keep your head down, except when looking up to wink and flirt with police.

Also, prepare to find new, creative, and useful roles for distant family members who may show up at your doorstep seeking shelter.

FOTKI

Photos are a big deal in a Russian household. This is the perfect way to flaunt your children's adept handling of guns and firearms, and your connected and wealthy friends.

When posing for photographs, think Beyonce baby announcement meets Russian mail order bride profile pic. Props are key. Take photos with flowers that are not in season (because you know people who have access to the international flower market). Take photos with Greek vases as a nod to Putin's amazing archaeological unearthing during one of his routine daily swims. Take photos with guns and near landmarks. It's best to hide in plain sight. Take photos in bathtubs with bottles of cognac. This will show that you are ready at any moment to entertain the authorities - even if they show up while you're bathing. Make sure you're posing in an exaggerated manner with all of these objects and always make a duck-pout face, like a 13-year-old with daddy issues or the President. Smiling is allowed only if you are lucky enough to have an admirable set of gold teeth. Don't hide those beauties!

In your home you must have a special table or shelf designated for framed photos from various parts of your life, especially birthdays, reunions, weddings, vacations, and the party when you got a new refrigerator (take this photo down if the police or nosy neighbors come over. They cannot know that you have working refrigeration. Hide the refrigerator under a large crop of dill). Do not ever display photos of a bar/bat mitzvah or a Jewish wedding. Unfortunately, you can't be Jewish anymore. Keep any Jewish memorabilia beneath the floorboards.

Once you come back from your latest cruise and organize all of your vacation photos on Picasaweb, you must immediately invite all of your friends over for a photo viewing party. The slideshow should be set to music; a mix of Russian folk from the 60s, club mixes of Adele and Bossa Nova tunes from Spotify. Of course, everyone will know that the cruise was just a carefully planned trip to exchange goods and information with other multi-nationalists. Make sure you include photos with "is it or isn't it" hand signals and props in the background so that your guests can put the pieces of the plot together without having to ask you any questions. It's best to communicate with your eyes, not your mouth.

SOCIAL ETIQUETTE

Contrary to what you're used to, use your middle finger to point at something, and your index finger to flip someone off. There are bound to be some misunderstandings. You will probably be pointing at someone and he will get irate that you're flipping him off. Calmly explain that you were not insulting him, you were simply identifying him to the secret police who want to take him down to Gitmo for some harmless questioning.

Hand signals should be used often. They are now key to communicating our alliances. Important: you start counting from "one" using your thumb. Thumbs-up no longer means "OK!" or "Terrific!" It's just the first digit in a calculation of the debt you owe your manicurist or dentist.

After any gathering - or just a quick visit to "drop something off" - it should always take you at least 30 minutes or longer to say goodbye when leaving someone's house. This is because while thanking your host you are carefully exchanging top-secret information via handshakes and coded hugs. Pat firmly on the back twice then once quickly for "abort mission."

Women:

Even if you are wearing a snowsuit covered from head to toe, you must be fully waxed with nails done. Eliminate all bodily hair, except for on your head. Don't carry any additional burdens because you'll need as many clean surface areas as possible to tape and smuggle goods on your body.

Don't smile.

Men:

You must wax your back, and have manscaped eyebrows, ears and neck. But keep your chest hairy to hide listening devices. Keeping up with this grooming routine is key to ensuring that all of your passport photos are consistent in appearance. Plus, it's easier to share passports with cousins when all of you look the same.

Don't smile.

PARANOIA

History buffs, you're in luck. The KGB is in style again! They can arrest you at any time, for anything or nothing at all. For this reason, paranoia is in the fiber of a Russian person's being.

Follow the **ABC** rule: **A**lways **B**e **C**autious.

Do not tell your children where you work. It doesn't matter if you have a job or not. Do not tell anyone what you do, how much money you make, where you keep the money. In fact, don't tell anybody anything. It can't be used against you in a court of law, because impartial courts are gone now, but it CAN be used against you in systemic government torture.

Prepare to answer questions with vague and neutral information, satisfying the inquiry, but not providing any actual answers. For example, if a coworker asks you about your family you should just smile, pause and say: "Thank you. Have you tried the beet chips from the vending machine?"

When visiting friends, make sure you park right in front of their building so they can see your shiny new car and then compliment you on it. When they compliment you, deny having a car. Walk away and don't get in the car. Later that night, have someone else come and drive away in the car.

MEDICAL: BECOMING YOUR OWN DOCTOR

Good news: Russian doctors are great!

Bad news: They have no resources or money and the hospitals are either corrupt or collapsing.

On top of hunting your own clothes and food to stay alive, consider learning some basic medical procedures like removing splinters, stitching wounds, and performing open heart surgery. On second thought, it's probably a good idea to stay healthy.

If you do get sick, see below.

Minor cuts

Disinfect with: vodka, black tea, honey or tobacco

Anesthetize with: vodka

Prevent infection with: vodka

Procedures & minor surgeries

Disinfect with: vodka, black tea, honey or tobacco

Anesthetize with: vodka

Prevent infection with: vodka

Tools: serrated knife from your track suit

Dental work like pulling your own tooth out

Disinfect with: vodka, black tea, honey or tobacco

Anesthetize with: vodka

Prevent infection with: vodka

Tools: pliers from your track suit

<u>Childbirth</u>

Disinfect with: black tea, honey or tobacco

Anesthetize with: sorry, nothing available

Tools: a sober family member to deliver the baby, clean wife-beater and the pocket knife from the tracksuit to cut the cord

<u>Major surgeries</u>
Hopefully you have connections. Good luck!

Depression & alcoholism are not acknowledged as medical conditions except by saying "he is very sick" or "he seemed very sad." The cure is simply some vigorous exercise, a trip to the mineral bath, and a dunk in the freezing sea.

Side note: If you're performing a blood transfusion, keep the borscht in another room to avoid mix-ups.

If we're lucky, some Soviet era medicine may soon return to the black market, like:

"Zelyonka" which loosely translates to "green stuff." Remember the dad from My Big Fat Greek Wedding and his obsession with Windex?

Zelyonka is basically the Windex of the Russian first aid kit. Nobody really knows exactly what is does, except dye your skin dark green like McCormick food coloring. But, it hasn't killed anyone (yet).

"Margantzovka" is a mysterious tiny crystal dust which dilutes in water turning into a mesmerizing purple, swirling liquid. It's used to treat nausea by making you throw up. It can be used to make a fancy-looking cocktail to throw your nemesis off course.

"Yeud" which is iodine has made every Soviet era child shriek in terror. It's dispensed out of an unmarked eye-dropper bottle and will lurk ominously in the back of the "secret" cupboard.

BONUS TIP

A cow is great to keep around the apartment, if you know where to steal one. It provides milk for the baby, dinner for dad, and leather pants for mom.

Chapter 2: Socializing with people you hate

From the minute you're born you will be surrounded by people you are obligated to love (but who give you every reason to hate them). Take heart, sycophants: flattery is easy once you get used to it and learn the right targets. This chapter will be your guide to parties, restaurants, vacations, reunions, weddings, funerals and more. Plus, you'll learn how to discern whom to sleep with and who may be spying on you, and the most important social aspect of being Russian: how to gossip and hold a grudge. Gossip and grudges will be key vehicles for casually spreading forbidden news, and for communicating vague threats.

SOCIALIZING AT HOME

To be Russian, you must acknowledge family as the most important part of your life. The cold weather is not the reason Russians are always drunk. It's family. Socializing at home isn't really a choice. You already live with all of your immediate family members plus some riff raff from the neighborhood in an apartment five times too small. It's why all the immigrants were kicked out of the country; so there'd be enough tenement housing for everyone who belongs here.

Every inch of your apartment will be put to communal use, from beds to TVs, open suitcases, clothes, ironing boards, photos, shot glasses, knick knacks, books, and shoes. View it as an in-house community recreational center. The kitchen doubles as a cafe for open mic night, where forbidden poetry and literature is read out loud. The NY Times has been applied to walls as extra wallpaper and insulation. You can catch up on real/fake news while you make eggplant ragu, and it's also very helpful for covering up any spy holes. The tray table in the living room is where you fix your eyeglasses, your children do their homework, you perform minor medical procedures, and hold chess tournaments. The bedroom is where the entire family sleeps, plus where you iron, sew, do calisthenics (deep squats, axe chops and kettle bells) and keep your extra grandmothers to prepare food.

It will become increasingly rare to receive surprise visitors as you once did. Even package deliveries will become more scarce, since there's too much security involved in scanning your latest order from Gap.com. You must become like a hawk, on constant watch. You will be sharing one set of keys with your entire family to ensure the highest measure of security and so an extra key is never lost. Everyone except the person who has access to the keys will be huddled at home combing through the composting to see if any hearty scraps were accidentally cast aside and figuring out what to serve for dinner. When they come home it's your turn to have the keys for two hours until you pass them onto your aunt who needs to visit that

17

ailing friend who still has access to great painkillers leftover from before the revolution.

FAMILY PARTIES

As a former American, you might be used to having family reunions once every census, perhaps somewhere in a nice wooded area with park benches, balloons, and a quiet space to be alone. Now that you're Russian, be prepared for weekly family reunions, every Saturday night, in a cramped Russian restaurant where you can smell your great-aunt's mothy polyester dress. If you don't live close to your family, be prepared to make a long trip for the reunion. You don't want them to wonder why you're such an asshole and hate your family, or if you're really "American" after all. The easiest thing to do is succumb and show up every Saturday night for whoever is having a birthday and act like it's the most unique party you've ever been to. Even though you saw all the same people last week, be prepared to answer questions with new and exciting information about your life.

It's helpful to always have a floor plan of your apartment or house on hand. Russian relatives love figuring out where they're going to live when they're on the lam (highly likely).

If you really can't make it, your only hope of not being ostracized is to call and wish whomever a Happy Birthday/Happy Anniversary/Happy Gall

Bladder Removal. Don't worry: you won't forget because you will receive text messages and voicemails from your mother reminding you to CALL SVETA in three days because it's her son's fifth grade graduation.

TOASTS AND ANECDOTES

No meal, celebration or gathering of any kind is complete without bountiful toasts and anecdotes. Prepare to spend 50% of every party listening or grimacing. *Everyone* is expected to speak and show their patriotism and love of family. Consider reciting all or part of a poem by Pushkin or a chant from good old Soviet summer camp. Make sure someone videotapes and puts it on YouTube so you have proof of your loyalty to the Motherland. Nobody will comment on the video (never let your opinions become part of the public record, even on social media), but it will have been forwarded over 1,000 times and have almost one million views in no time.

Only the brave - or those with no skills at all - will tell anecdotes ("anekdoti"). The way to tell an anecdote is to interrupt the conversation and just start loudly telling it. This rule applies to any dinner party conversation. Make sure you're always interrupting someone because what you have to say is always more important. This will help cement you into the Russian culture.

Russians are the masters (and possibly the creators) of bravado. They tend to think whatever they're saying is true, so you should assume the same, especially if they say it louder than everyone else. For example, someone in the Russian government might say "We didn't hack the election" while a journalist working on the story for three years might say "You definitely hacked the election and we have proof." Pick your favorite truth, clear your throat, and yell over everyone. No one will doubt that you belong.

CHECKLIST BEFORE GOING TO A PARTY

I.   Bleached blonde or eggplant-colored hair (the eggplant hue is YUGE in Russia. We eat it, we wear it, we paint our faces with it. Just go with it).

II.   Lip-liner that almost reaches your chin.

III. An obvious wig or exaggerated hair extensions in a shade 10 times lighter or darker than your natural hair.

IV.   Cleavage that's tight enough to cradle a knife, a vile of poison, a written-out toast, a gun, an encrypted message, a lighter or an envelope.

V. 50% of your outfit should be encrusted in Swarovski crystals (great place to hide a camera). Even though you're poor, you're not a peasant! You'll always have that one "special" dress, that you'll share with your aunt/cousin/best friends or whomever is on spy circuit that night.

Men:

Be very inappropriate with your friends' daughters, nieces, goddaughters and any woman you've known since birth.

Women:

Accept getting sexually harassed by your uncle or father's best friend, because you'll need him to storm out of the car dealership tomorrow when he's helping you negotiate a car purchase. You can deal with it later in therapy. Just kidding! Therapy's over now. So is quality healthcare in general. And human rights.

GIFTS

Always show up to parties with an enormous envelope of cash, an oversized box of chocolates and flowers, and give everything to the host directly. For a successful exchange, they need to acknowledge how fat the envelope is so when they come to your birthday next month, their envelope is fatter.

If you receive something that's not cold hard cash or vodka, cognac, or tequila, throw it out immediately because it's probably bugged.

If a friend or cousin is travelling somewhere you have relatives - including distant 4th cousins - you must send a gift for them, even if both parties don't know each other, and you haven't ever met them (you probably haven't). This is referred to as "Russian UPS," the only postal service Russians trust. For example, if you're going to visit New York from Boston, you will most likely get a call from your aunt that she wants to send a box of adult diapers, Tylenol, and a book to her mother's elderly friend in Philadelphia. Philadelphia is not on the way to New York, but don't try to argue; otherwise this stranger's blood is on your hands. This is a symptom of not trusting the system. Look around. Have you ever met a Russian UPS guy? You have. Because they're ALL UPS guys.

URA & URA TAX

"Soveti" means "advice" in Russian. If it looks like an anagram for "Soviet," you're not wrong. Thinly masked insults from your relatives are known as **U**nsolicited **R**ussian **A**dvice. Russian URAs will be dispensed at any given moment without any warning and there's no way to prevent or predict them. Be prepared at every family gathering, wedding, baby shower and birthday party, especially at *your* birthday party. This seems to be the optimal time for every guest to kiss you on the cheek while groping you, congratulate you, ask how you're doing and then BOOM: URA.

A URA can go something like this:

"Congratulations on your new job! You know, if you really want to be successful you should talk to my son Vadik who has good connections for computer programmer job."

"If you're really serious about losing weight you should call my cousin Sveta. She has Herbalife connections."

URAs will make you smile, then cry. But, do you remember that thick envelope full of cash? That's your URA Tax. URA Tax is the unspoken agreement between comrades and cousins. It's like helping your opponent up after knocking them out in three rounds. It only makes us stronger.

INSULTS & COMEBACKS

Russian people are not known for being discreet. Forget everything you know about being a passive-aggressive American. Now you get to say what you think to people's faces—as long as they are not military, the police or elected officials. In a culture of distrust, if you don't insult everyone you are close to, it will appear very suspicious. Some politicians have been using this method of communication for years, while others are just getting their footing. Insults are a great way to distract the opposition, especially when they are not expecting it. Even more reason to sharpen these skills! And, to identify those insulted so you can reach out and forge new alliances.

Insult: "Your apartment is so nicely decorated. I guess that's one positive to having a gay son." Comeback: *Smile, kiss on cheek, and walk away.* Do not confirm or deny, but offer design help when you learn that they have a cousin in government.

I: "Are you smuggling something under that blouse or did you gain weight?"
C: "I'm gaining weight to keep up with you."

I: "You're visiting HER in the labor camps? I had no idea you socialized with Jews."
C: "Feeling guilty because I bring her better snacks than you bring your own son?"

I: "You look nice in that dress even though red is not your color."
C: "Red is everyone's color now."

RUSSIAN RESTAURANTS

The following events are considered milestones and must be held in a gilded function hall or a Russian restaurant. It's all about gold, gold, gold, gold, gold, gold, gold. And platinum. And diamonds.

-       20th, 25th, 30th, 35th, 40th, 45th, 50th, 55th, 60th, 65th, 70th, 75th, 80th, 85th, 90th, and 95th birthday.

-       1st, 5th, 10th, 15th, 20th, 25th, 30th, 35th, 40th, 45th, 50th, 55th, 60th wedding anniversary.

-       High school graduation, college graduation, grad school graduation, medical/dental/law school graduation, labor camp release.

As a guest it's imperative to dress in Russian Black-Tie. Wear enough makeup and jewelry that you tip the scale up by at least ten pounds (this applies to men and women). Arrive in your most expensive fur or leather.

Smoke a cigarette between parking the car and entering the restaurant. You'll run into everyone else invited to the party also smoking near the entrance. Welcome to the new American tailgate. Unlike tailgates of the past, this event is not festive, but an opportunity to find out who at the party is an informer, who is undercover KGB, what waiters are working and what they're serving for dinner. This is also a good time to exchange microchips, settle minor cash debts, and tip each other off to critical information such as where to get the best caviar for the best price (free).

Once you have the information you may make your entrance. Service will be slow now that all the immigrants have been deported. While you wait for the main course, scan the room by slowly turning left and right as though you're nodding at people. Really you're capturing everything on film in the camera that's hidden in your Swarovski crystals.

You and your spouse should develop eye signals to indicate who you should flirt with. For example, if your husband goes outside with someone for a cigarette, that's a signal that he's a high-ranking government official and you should flirt with him on the dance floor later on. This is all for the greater good and safety of your family. You can never have too many friends in government. If your husband goes out for a second cigarette with the same person this is a signal that your life is danger and you must vacate the premises within five minutes.

HOW TO SOCIALIZE WITH ENEMIES OF THE STATE

It is not recommended to socialize with people wanted by the government, but it's considered heroic amongst members of the resistance. Enemies include: traitors, people accused of treason, gays, Jews, journalists, artists who took it too far, musicians, bartenders (they ruined vodka), Snapchat, anyone from the Obama administration, anyone named Hillary, and anyone wearing or knitting a Pussy Power hat. Pussies are for grabbing, only.

It's very likely that you'll encounter many of these people whether or not you try to avoid them. Your best move is to learn how to handle them with ease, especially if they come knocking on your door. If you live on the ground floor or the top floor of your building, you may be asked to hide Jews or gays under your trap door or in your attic. Though you're better off keeping your distance you should first consider: what's in it for me? Don't forget that everything can be bartered and sold, even what used to be known as freedom! If someone needs to use your apartment or office as a safe house make sure you're getting a proper payout. Forget about old American feel-good philanthropy. Now, the only acceptable thing to say is: show me the money! But, don't report the money.

Even though you should not generally be helping out any marginalized group, Jews and gays are the only ones you should go out on a limb for; that is if they're good looking and they can get you a good deal on diamonds, a lifetime supply of challah, or mix a good cocktail. You can be sure they'll suddenly find a bunch of cash when you remind them that their lives are on the line. Sweeten the deal by giving them a few blankets to cushion the cement floor beneath the floorboards or in the closet.

Old world philanthropy and non-for-profit giving is out the window. From now on you will be helping the greater good but by staying smart and appearing committed to the cause. Don't ever reveal that you may not support the new administration. Just like George Costanza, if *you* believe it then it *is* the truth. Don't worry: when this all blows over in a few years (or tomorrow) it will be just as easy to switch over to a new truth. By then you'll be adept at assuming timely identities and convenient political platforms.

In the meantime, Fox News should be on in every room of the house so there is never any doubt about your alliances. If you find yourself at the rare gala or benefit make sure you have pamphlets about Putin to hand out and that your gay friends can be reached immediately for a costume change if you need to go undercover.

GYM

The gym or bathhouse (Banya) is a great place to pay homage to the President by parading around shirtless. You must put in several weekly appearances in order to track who in your circle can out-lift you, outrun you, and knock you down. Don't let it get to this point; you must always throw the last punch.

The gym is also the perfect place to smuggle and trade goods, and meet up with your "team." Use gym implements as props and communication tools. Kettle bells, which were used in old Russia to weigh grain, were developed into a weight-lifting system and can be used to communicate messages using the symbols on each weight. Lift the 10lb weight to signal you've acknowledged your accomplice, 15lb to signal that it's time to move on the mission (retrieve duffle bag from locker 15), and the 20lb weight when the mission is accomplished (and, they have 20 minutes to hand off the duffel bag). You can also sneak code words into those groans and grunts.

The gym is basically your office and mothership for operations. Here you can hold "meetings" under the guise of working out as a personal trainer. When your enemy disagrees with you, add 100lbs to their chest press mid-air and they will surely be saying "UNCLE." Mission accomplished, and on to the rowing machine.

If they fail to see things your way, approach them in the shower and give them a second chance to surrender. If they still don't go along with your request they're very, very stupid, because it's very, very hard to investigate a crime that may or not have taken place in the shower, where evidence can just wash away...

After you have a nice steam to clean your pores don't forget to visit the cafe. Your hard day's work should always be rewarded with a carafe of vodka and a smoked fish platter.

GROOMING

Waxing, skincare, hairdos and manicures are a right of passage for Russians and can start as early as age eight (especially waxing). Most likely, you'll be related to your nail lady, frenemies with your aesthetician, and roommates with your wax lady. The latter is convenient because a lot of Russian wax ladies conduct business in their bedrooms.

Women:

Perfectly dyed eyebrows are a status symbol and show you can pivot to becoming a stripper or prostitute if duty calls. Waxing is important to keep the body clean of excess hair. The less hair, the less painful it will be when you remove wiretap tape. Also, your wax lady can give you information which will be covered with your screams.

A standard cut and color offers ample time to gossip, bitch and complain. It's not too different from an American hair salon, except you're in the hairdresser's bathroom or kitchen. Your hairdresser is also a florist on the side. Conveniently, her husband is an allergist.

Nails are done by the hairdresser while you're waiting for your color to set. Russian women don't bother with certificates or licenses. Thanks to evolution, they're just born with these survival skills. Should you need to alter your appearance and identity, it's always good to know a Russian woman. She can whip up a "brand new you" in no time.

Men:
A man must enter every party, office, and restaurant preceded by his cologne by 10 minutes, and leave the same lingering scent for at least twenty minutes after he has departed. Cologne intoxicates women into lightheadedness making them more likely to tolerate you, while distracting everyone else with a headache. This will give you a chance to survey the room and check in with your "people" who have arrived ahead of you.

Hair should be trimmed bi-weekly for grooming purposes but also because your barber - who is also your cousin - has to keep you informed about his end of the family business. He is also the only one who can trim around your hair while you keep your Bluetooth on, because you NEVER take off the Bluetooth. Ever.

If you skip your scheduled trim you can wear a cap or a fedora, but never a baseball hat unless it's leather Versace, Gucci, Fendi or ADIDAS. Seek clothes and overcoats by deceased Italian designers, so as to better blend in.

SOCIAL MEDIA

To keep up appearances, you must learn how to create and maintain a believable social media presence, peppering in your political views so that your enemies and allies know where you stand.

Just for good measure, here are some do's & don'ts:

DO

- Share an article praising Putin. Make sure he's shirtless in the photo.

- Post a private message for your daughter on your own wall without tagging her. Angrily call her 10 minutes later and ask her why she never answered you.

- Share Breitbart articles about family values.

- "Like" all 193 of your son's ex-wife's 2nd wedding photos (she works for a high-level official).

- Post an amateur clip art ad for your taxi service which includes your home phone number (this is a way to appear transparent). When someone calls the phone number always have your grandmother answer to screen the calls.

- Instagram a photo of your second cousin's neighbor in a bathtub with a bottle of cognac.

- Re-post a screenshot of a proverb written in oversized font and heavily pixelated from repeated reproduction.

DON'T

- Post anything against Putin. Even if he's shirtless in the photo.

CULTURE

Arts and culture are the cornerstone of the Russian experience; they thrive under oppression (just like the resistance). Cultured gatherings are also a great place to plot and plan (think Baryshnikov in "White Nights"). Go to the ballet, go to the opera, go to the theater, go to the movies, go to museums, read books, watch the news (FOX - duh). Go often and as much as you like. But of course, when those directors, singers, dancers, writers and artists get arrested for being traitors or when journalists are assassinated for doing their jobs, say "Good riddance." Say it loudly so your neighbors can hear you.

If you must absorb banned literature do it in a group: there's safety in numbers. Cram right into the kitchen with your sleeping uncle and read books and poetry aloud to each other. Make sure to turn on your noise machine. Maybe have one of your guests face the window and sing the Russian national anthem for two hours straight for extra safety measures. If your neighbor does catch you reading banned books, make sure you have something over her. Blackmail is key to survival. When they come by, always be generous and serve salted herring with onions, black bread, vodka, tea with sour cherry jam. Never miss a chance to feed them, and feed them well, otherwise they'll gossip about you for not offering refreshments.

GOSSIP

Russian gossip is the original alternative facts. Gossip and grudges are dispensed and maneuvered in a way to throw people off course and send society into a spiral of confusion, anger, and distrust. The only way out of it is to spread new information via gossip and grudges. It's a self-perpetuating cycle of adapted information, a skill you must master if you wish to survive on the cold steppe of this administration.

Gossip is a fine art in Russian culture and nothing is off limits. If someone is not in the room, they're fair game. Discuss their clothes. Discuss their upbringing. Discuss their American husband (in disgust, but then find out if he comes from money and if he can be hit up for an occasional "loan"). Discuss their house. Discuss their hair. Discuss their décor. Discuss what they did or didn't serve you for dinner. Discuss their money, how they got it, where they keep it, and when they're going to share it with you. Discuss their friend's kid's cousins, and extended family, potential matchmaking and how it will benefit you.

The kind American expression "Bless their heart!" will be replaced with the Russian version, "Well, good luck to them." If that person actually succeeds later on you must act surprised and fake happy and then try to get in on the profit sharing.

When discussing your neighbor's life (ideally on a park bench), leave no stone unturned. But also come to no conclusion. Gossip is a lifelong pursuit with no degree. The gossip game of two old Russian women is one the rest of us can only strive for. This is why Russians live so long. They never fully achieve their gossip goals so they always have something to wake up for.

There's nothing too big or too small to hold a grudge for. This includes but is not limited to:
1. Not being complimented on your lipstick.

2. Someone else being complimented on their shoes.

3. Someone else's kids getting a scholarship even though their kids' SAT scores were worse.

4. Your grandson's fiancée not trying your pickled herring at dinner (even though she ate three plates of food and came from another party).

5. Your neighbor not asking how you're feeling after a routine physical.

6. Your sister's daughter getting engaged before your daughter (even though your daughter is 12).

7. Your cousin's sons birthday is on the same day as your son's: that's not okay.

8. Your coworker claims to have "discovered" a Russian cafe that you've been going to for 15 years (and is owned by your family).

9. Your fourth cousin's granddaughter not calling to wish you congratulations on your son's birthday, even though he is turning 37. Even more important than personally wishing someone a Happy Birthday is calling their parents to congratulate *them*.

TRAVEL (SPYING)

If you're feeling fenced in, that's because there's a fence being built around your country. But it also might mean it's time for a vacation!

Russian people love to travel. It has something to do with the whole not-being-let-out-of-Russia-for-80-years thing.

Tips for appearing Russian while leaving the country (for civilians and spies):

1. Complain. This is key. Russian people have had bad luck for centuries and there's a lot of trauma underneath those

tough exteriors. Complaining about everything and anything shows you're not willing to look inside for what's really wrong, like a real Russian person.

2. Always have a return ticket. If not, you'll be shot on the spot.

3. You're going for work. You're ALWAYS going for work. No country is better than Russia. You are NOT going for pleasure. There is not pleasure to be found anywhere but where you are.

Tips for appearing Russian while in another country:

1. Complain

Tips for appearing Russian while coming back through Customs:

1. Complain about the terrible trip you had and how happy you are to be home.

2. Have a big photo party when you return and invite all of your friends and family over.

None of this is that important, because soon you won't be able to travel anywhere. Or take pictures.

Jews:

Passport stamped with "Jew."

If you're not white, Christian or secular Russian you'll need to reapply for a special visa even to cross state lines. To speed this process along make sure you've got your NRA sticker clearly displayed. This will confirm at least one satisfactory alliance and increase your chances of getting past state checkpoints.

HOLIDAYS

New Year's

New Year's in the first and biggest celebration of the year because it commemorates an older man with a much, much younger woman at his side. Ded Moroz, "Grandfather Winter," is the hero of the holiday and he is assisted by that slut Snegurachka,"The Snow Maiden." Thus, the first day of every year gives hope to all the toothless single old men as well as to the young, single, and desperate young women trying to find a "better" life.

Russian Christmas, January 7

Russian Christmas is based on the old Julian calendar, hence the date, but many of the traditions of caroling and festivities are similar.

There used to be a custom of young women telling fortunes. However most of these young women have found it impossible to keep up with the unpredictability of daily life, or they've been imprisoned. In Soviet times even Christmas was abolished but still secretly celebrated by many people. Nowadays religion is a very convenient resource for when the government wants to arrest people (Pussy Riot).

Man's Day, February 23 (and every day)

Until recently, this holiday was known as Soviet Army Day. Nowadays it's a holiday for all men, young and old, to be praised as eventual defenders. Basically, men get praised for maybe eventually doing something to help their country whether or not they're actually going to defend anyone. Sound familiar?

Women's Day, March 8

This is the only day of the year that your husband will definitely not beat you. It's actually quite sacred and joyful, knowing that you're safe on this day until midnight! However, between March 9th and March 7th we cannot make any guarantees that your spouse won't use his legalized once-a-year smackdown.

Maslenitsa "Pancake Week"

Long ago this holiday signified the end of winter and beginning of spring. Games, food — pancakes with caviar, of course — and festivities abounded, ending in the ritual burning of a scarecrow. But in recent times, perhaps due to limited resources or flagging spirits, most families celebrate simply by eating pancakes whilst watching news reporting on the latest "mysterious" and "accidental" deaths. Once four mysterious deaths have occurred, the end of winter is official and a fresh batch of batter is mixed! Rumor has it the burning of an orange scarecrow is having a resurgence.

Russian Orthodox Easter

Christ has risen! And then we never saw him again.

May Day, May 1

Centuries ago this was a widely celebrated holiday known as International Solidarity of Workers, and was marked by parades, balloons, and festivities. More recently it lost its ideological meaning and was eventually renamed the Holiday of Spring and Work. Basically, this means that it's Springtime — so clean up your shit and get back to work.

Victory Day, May 9

This holiday epitomizes Russian culture because it's somehow both joyful and mournful all at once. Remember: *just* joy is unacceptable without pain and suffering. That's why our May 9th victory over fascist Germany in 1945 is a solemn holiday. But we do get the day off work and the occasional military parade, once every five or 10 years. They celebrate the holiday whenever they feel like it and when we haven't "lost" too many key figures that year. This holiday has been updated to include the Russian victory of the United States Presidential Election.

The Day of National Unity, November 4

In 2005, in a desperate move to up their game in the holiday department, Russia revived a victory over Poland from 1612. This now marks our so-called "Day of National Unity" commemorating Russia's victory over Polish invaders. Poland will forever be Russia's shorter, fatter, and stupider cousin and now everyone knows it.

BONUS TIP

Things that are okay: black tea, black bread, black leather pants.
Things that are not okay: black friends.

Chapter 3: Don't be political!

This is going to be a tough transition. All those fun American things you're used to like freedom of speech, choosing who to vote for, having control over your own body, and mocha Frappuccino's, are gone. The former (current) head of the KGB is in charge now, so you need to start paying attention…to everything. Train your ear to pick up on plots, plans and revolutionaries. Don't forget that while you're eavesdropping on them, they're eavesdropping on you.

DISCERNING HIDDEN MESSAGES IN STATE-RUN MEDIA

The following examples and incidents are coincidental. They do not at all relate to political activism, voicing of opinion, or speaking out against the government or in support of a cause*. You must understand that a lot of Russian deaths *are* mysterious, accidental, unexpected, unexplainable, and coincidental. It's a feature of our nationality. So you mustn't be too shocked if your new Russian family members show evidence of:

1. Poisoning
2. Mysterious illness
3. Assassination
4. Missing kettle bells
5. Disappearance
6. Exile
7. Imprisonment

8. Torture
9. Torn velour tracksuit or fur
10. Illegal searches
11. Death threats
12. Cracked (and hacked) cell phone with new Putin wallpaper background
13. Frequent falling out of windows (one time shame on me, two times shame on the KGB)
14. Finding a bloody bear claw in your bed
15. Being sprayed with permanent green paint (or "zelenka")

This was a test to see if you were able to discern the "hidden" meaning. If it all looked normal to you, keep reading.

A DAY IN THE LIFE OF AN APOLITICAL PERSON

If the above incidents look fine to you, it means you've drunk the Kvas (Russian kool-aid) and are perfectly happy living a life controlled by a fascist regime. Being apolitical will work well for you, but might get you in trouble if the regime gets overthrown. In the meantime, to avoid "accidental" poisoning or mysteriously shredded fur, your life will be spent dodging incrimination.

If you're not political, your day might go something like this:

6am: You're the first one up (or are you?) and you hear a scream from the street. Close the window and make your tea.

6:20am: Turn on the news. If they're reporting about yet another unsolved murder of a Pulitzer prize winning humanitarian journalist, turn on some music to drown it out, and whistle along. If, on cue, a text from your friend comes through: "Did you see the news?! Can you believe this?! WTF," throw your phone in the toilet, flush, and prepare to make new friends (again). Open the bathroom cabinet to retrieve your toothbrush and your next burner phone (the sim cards are next to your razors).

6:45am: Dressing for work you may find you a wire tap in your sock drawer. Start humming the national anthem directly into the sock drawer as you're knotting your tie.

7:15am: On your way to work you pass a group with pamphlets and signs peacefully trying to gather a protest group. Look the other way: protesting is illegal. If you need to get into the good graces of the authorities you may want to report this group (even though it could just be a school field trip to the museum). Nobody is too young to go to jail and any act of solidarity with the government will be well regarded on your record.

8:00am: On the metro, always be a patriot! If someone asks how you feel about the president, say "He's super!" and remember to smile.

8:15 am: You're getting off the metro and someone in front of you drops a leather glove. Walk on without alerting them to lost glove. You never know: this might be a signal they're sending to someone nearby to complete a transaction. You don't want to jeopardize a potentially crucial mission that has deep roots in an international hacking plot.

8:30 am: You arrive at your office only to find your coworker being interrogated by the secret police. This is a typical daily occurrence. Don't make eye contact, but if you do just give the universal eye nod, and get to your desk and look busy even if you have nothing to do. The important thing is to appear engrossed, but really you should be eavesdropping on the adjacent interrogation. You'll need to know how to answer the same questions tomorrow when they show up for you.

11:00am: News comes in that the President has invaded yet another country and stripped the rights of even more citizens. Now is a good time to use the bathroom.

11:05am: Bathroom break.

1:00pm: Lunch! You can go out to a cafe with your co-workers for the typical two-hour break. But if your company has a cafeteria, you should consider eating there as often as possible in order to avoid suspicion. Not eating on premises might be construed as a signal that you're engaged in suspicious activity. It's also an insult to the cafeteria chef. Stay on his good side. You'll need him for rations.

3:00pm: If you haven't been abducted and blindfolded in the backseat of a town car, congratulations! Now, get back to work. You've got to clock another two hours before the day is over.

5:00pm: Make sure you leave work not a minute early or late. If you linger a co-worker may suspect that you're abusing the office for your side projects or activism.

5:30pm: You walk by where the protesters were gathered and notice the area has been taped off and is under surveillance.

6:00pm: You arrive home after this typical day. You hear your neighbors across the way singing the national anthem out the window. This can only mean one thing: they've gathered to read poetry and play the guitar. Make a mental note, or jot it down in code in your journal. This is crucial for negotiation tactics later on.

6:30pm: Dinner is served (by your mother. Remember: your entire family is living together). Dinner conversation should be limited to marveling at Putin's latest shirtless appearance and why your son didn't show up for dinner.

7:00 pm: Turns out your son was arrested for protesting in that very same taped-off spot from earlier today. You make sure to scream "That's no son of mine" into your sock drawer.

8:00 pm: Watch the evening news for about an hour. It's a mix of Putin praise, Putin is great, Putin is not a gay clown, Russia is great, other countries are evil, Russian men are the best, Russian women need to be feminine, why should gays have rights?, Putin is amazing, and some commercials for soap and where to wait in line for it the next day at 5 am.

9:00 pm: Wind down by putting your ear to the wall and listening to more of your neighbor's "poetry." Write down or record any key phrases like "we need to do something," "Jews are people too," "what happened to Democracy?" and "Meryl Streep is an American treasure." This kind of talk is frowned upon and great fodder for the police. The more info you have to deflect the blame onto others, the better.

10:00 pm: Listen to some appropriate music (Adele, Justin Timberlake, or Jennifer Lopez are all fine) and work on the list for your birthday next month. You have to cross-reference and remove anyone who's spoken out against the system or been recently wiretapped. But that's fine, as you'll find that many have been suffering from "unexplainable illnesses" from which they may or may not recover. So feel free to cross them off the list. Forever.

SPYING ON, AND REPORTING, YOUR NEIGHBORS

If you've been approached by the authorities because they are "on to you," the first thing you must do is ensure that you have secured the trust of your neighbors and the entire extended family living with them. Always cast your net wide. Especially if your alliance with the police is in question, you should start befriending everyone around you: the local bartender, your mailman, the garbage man (this will come in handy later), your children's teachers and a few key classroom parents such as a lawyer, a doctor, a dentist, a musician, and a chef (preferably none of these people are Jewish anymore). Now that you've forged these relationships you can report back on them to the KGB in exchange for immunity or to be allowed to keep your cable and internet (still with limited access to just FOX and Breitbart and a dubbed Mexican telenovela).

You should always be looking for ways to spy on your neighbors, friends and family. Chances are they've already got a file on you, so don't fall behind! You should have all your evidence and ammo at the ready in case the police show up for an unannounced raid.

FAKE NEWS

Fox, Breitbart, or RT: have them on your TV, download the apps, keep an iPad with the apps open in every room of your house. Print out articles from the Fox, Breitbart, and RT websites to give out to your friends. Don't forget to forward articles to everyone on your email server.

To round out your knowledge of current events, be sure to pick up the very popular and widely circulated Russian printed newspaper Novoye Ruskoye Slovo, which translates to New Russian Word (of Mouth). Even though this newspaper was established in 1910 in the US, you can be sure it's just a bunch of articles written by your cousins and uncles used to widely circulate information. The information is in the letters and symbols: think "A Beautiful Mind."

Your local Russian Bulletin, which is basically the Russian "Time Out," is another good resource, where you'll find ads for Russian lawyers, doctors and masseurs alongside ads for ballroom dancing studios, specialty food importing, and funeral homes. Should you need them there are plenty of computer programmers available for hire here, slotted between the ads for farmer's cheese and

Italian furniture and fashion stores on Brighton Beach. Most of this furniture already comes equipped with wire taps.

WHAT TO DO WHEN YOUR LOVED ONES DISAPPEAR

When your family disappears, don't be surprised: be grateful! You'll have so many distant cousins, uncles and aunts squatting in various parts of your home, you won't even notice when someone goes missing. This is the hazard and benefit of communal living. Everyone is expendable, except your uncle on the cot. Keep a close eye on him, while he is keeping a close eye on everyone.

BEING POLITICAL (SHHHH)

Almost daily, you're confronted with disturbing headlines about someone gone missing, or mysteriously poisoned. These messages include: "The death was deemed an 'accident.'" "Her disappearance was 'unexpected.'" "His sudden illness is 'unexplainable and untreatable.'" Any time this phraseology is used you must deconstruct. Here is what they are really saying: he was killed by the government for stating his opinion or doing his job.

A DAY IN THE LIFE OF A POLITICAL PERSON

6 am: You're the first one up and you hear a scream from the street. You open the window to see if everyone's alright. Nobody's alright. You throw on your coat and run down the stairs. By the time you get outside, everyone has scattered except for a man on the corner who's talking on his cell phone and looking directly at you.

6:15 am: You're back home and you turn on the news. They're reporting about an unsolved murder of a Pulitzer Prize winning humanitarian journalist. You text your friend: "Did you see the news?! Can you believe this?! WTF." Your friend writes back "Who dis?"

6:45 am: You're dressing for your protest. Jeans, sneakers, winter coat and a pussy hat to go with the pussy riot. Since there's no real women's movement in Russia, you'll probably be out there by yourself, maybe with one or two other people. You'll find a wire tap in your sock drawer. Lean in close and say "go fuck yourselves."

7:00 am: You try to post about the protest, but Facebook keeps turning your post into a photo of the beloved Russian bear "Cheburashka." You deactivate your Facebook account and open a new one, where you try to unsuccessfully post about the protest again.

7:00 am: You're on your way to the illegal protest (they weren't able to obtain the obscenely expensive permits).

7:15 am: You're at the protest. There are four other people there. You're arrested immediately.

3:00 pm: You've been blindfolded for seven hours and think you're in the back of a van but you're not sure.

Three weeks later: Life at the Siberian labor camp isn't as bad as it was last year! You're meeting nightly with your secret women's group. Your friend (the gay guy you've been hiding in your apartment) has made the trek to bring you Kit Kats and Kvas. Just 708 more days until freedom!

INTERROGATIONS

Should you find yourself in an interrogation room being asked to give up your friends, here's a script you should follow closely.

Apolitical:

Write down every name you know and tell them there's more where that came from. Hum the Russian National Anthem while you write. Circle the temples, mosques and gay clubs on the local map of your neighborhood.

Political:

"Let's cut through the shit. Just send me to the labor camp. I forgot my pen last time I was there anyway."

CENSORSHIP

There's a silver lining to censorship: money! Russian hackers are amazing at finding banned movies and TV shows and streaming them on illegal sites on the dark internet. Not only will you be able to enjoy entertainment at no extra expense, but if you meet the right people, you can even get paid to distribute it! Don't let the Chinese dubbing ruin your movie watching experience. If the actors are good, you'll be able to understand what's going on through their facial expressions. This will soon be part of the common core curriculum.

SURVEILLANCE ON THE GO

Russians long ago mastered the art of surveillance on the go. This is best exemplified on the boardwalk of Coney Island and other urban and suburban pathways. You'll see two old men or two old ladies strolling in what appears to be a casual conversation, but they're actually providing landlocked backup to the coast guard. From their vantage point along the shore they are the first ones to spot the submarine eyes of the ocean. Like all Russians they are playing both sides (shhh). Patrolling the shore under the guise of socializing is also the perfect way to assist their comrades in smuggling goods in and out of various ports.

Like an MLB catcher and pitcher with hands clasped behind their backs they are able to dispense an entire playbook of hand signals. Glancing up they are signaling to their teams on land and shore. If you ever see these groups walking at a normal pace you should run and hide. They only speed up when it's time to diffuse a situation or get themselves out of harm's way.

All along the boardwalk they have teams of back-up who are disguised as groups of men engrossed in chess tournaments. Actually, some of them really are playing chess. But the rest of the lot is in on the spy game. You will rarely meet a Russian who does not play chess. This is some of the earliest training you receive in life, and like everything else, it has to serve at least a dual purpose otherwise it is rendered useless. To be Russian you can't just enjoy something for its face value. Faces have no value. Only vodka, favors, and cash currency.

HIDING JEWS AND HAVING GAY FRIENDS

The Nazi party is still calling themselves the Alt Right. Cute. Once they take over and re-instate concentration camps, you may have some interesting choices to make. To hide Jews or not to hide Jews? If you choose to be a hero, hiding them in plain sight is best. Dye their hair blonde, get them blue contacts and new passports (from your cousin), and put them on a cot in your living room. They'll fit right in! If you're black, gay, Muslim or disabled, you're going to have to live in disguise (see above).

CHURCH AND STATE

Russian people have recently reconnected with religion. The government uses this regularly in its favor. Putin seems to have rediscovered the value of using religion in a time of crises and unearthing early religious roots after a few life-threatening incidents in his own life. Now he wants to make religion a compulsory part of the school curriculum so that youngsters can learn early that no matter what you do wrong, you can always ask the church for forgiveness by finding an obscure passage absolving you of your crimes. This should be an easy transition for Catholics.

Dissident or not, you'll need to learn the following political terms to survive:

Recuse

Espionage

Blue jeans

Censorship

Nationalism

Clandestine

Patrick Swayze

Bribe

Bolshoi Ballet

Edward Snowden

Stay quiet

Pussy Riot

Meryl Streep

Fetters

Reagan

Bruce Willis

Wire tapp

Hacker

Leonardo DiCaprio

Everything's super!

Pride

Country before family

Siphon

BONUS TIP

What to have in your GO-bag: vinegar, handkerchief, cash, Russian coffee cake "Pryanik" and Bruce Willis movies (the KGB loves him).

Chapter 4: Romantic Relationships

"If he hits you, it means he loves you." - Russian proverb

It's your lucky day, if you're a straight, white man! The Russian government just decriminalized domestic violence. How fortunate, because this aligns exactly with the former United States of America's stripping away of women's rights.

First things first.

THE BASICS

If you're a woman, you must get married by the time you're 24. You do not want to reach 25 as a spinster. It's a dark place. If you're a man, you can stay single as long as you want and your mother will shoo away her judgmental friends by telling them you're a "true professional pursuing his dreams who hasn't met a woman who deserves him yet, but boy is she tired of doing his laundry and cooking so hopefully he'll meet someone soon so that she moves in and takes over all of the unpaid, unappreciated housework."

Don't worry: they'll never suspect you're gay if you're unmarried. Being gay will *always* be worse than not marrying and producing grandchildren. You should point this out whenever your mother complains that you don't even separate your darks and whites (unlike some people).

A Russian woman's middle name is always her father's first name, with an "a" at the end, to indicate she belongs to him. When she gets married, she keeps her father's first name as her middle name and loses her father's last name to replace with her husband's last name, also with an "a" at the end, to indicate she now also belongs to him. This is quite confusing for a newcomer.

In short: A woman belongs to her father until she gets married, whereupon she belongs to her husband more.

For example: Gorbachev's wife's name was "Raisa Gorbacheva." The "a" indicates she is "of Gorbachev." It's kind of like indentured servitude without a release date (except death).

Staying fertile is a must. A Russian person (woman) is nothing without offspring. A Russian person (woman) has no purpose other than breeding (plus cooking, cleaning, working in the field she went to college for and bearing the responsibility for her husband's alcoholism, debts, and poorly timed joke-telling).

What to do if you fall in love with someone who's not white:
Not recommended. Move to Canada.

Where to hide if you're gay:
Manhattan.

How to satisfy your in-laws if you're a man:
Impregnate their daughter and fix their
computer.

How to satisfy your in-laws if you're a woman:
You can't.

The most important thing about having a
relationship with someone is that they're of the
opposite sex and white.

ROMANCE LESSONS FROM RUSSIAN ARTS AND HISTORY

We can learn a lot about romance and the role of
women in relationships by taking a stroll through
literature and Soviet history. Russian literature is
much like marriage; it starts with a fever and ends
with a premature death.

THE ARTS

1) *Anna Karenina* by Leo Tolstoy

> That slut Anna Karenina throws herself
> in front of a train because she dared to

follow her heart and make a fool out of her husband.

Lesson: If you make a fool out of a man, you deserve nothing less than death.

2) *War & Peace* by Leo Tolstoy

That slut Natasha falls in love with Andrei, but then he decides to be a fucking hero and fight in the war so she jumps in bed with Anatole who's run out of town by her slut-shaming mother. She ends up with Pierre after Pierre's wife overdoses and Andrei dies of heartbreak (and battle wounds).

Lesson: You can get what you want at the expense of your loved ones dying.

3) *The Death of Ivan Ilyich* by Fyodor Dostoyevsky

Ivan Ilyich is a respectable man with an annoying and boring wife (if only she were a slut). He falls while hanging a curtain one day and hits his side. Next thing he knows he's dying and hates his wife more than ever. In his very last moments on earth, he realizes she's not *that* bad.

Lesson: Your wife can be forgiven and loved, but only when you're dying and don't have to spend time with her anymore.

4) *Eugene Onegin* by Alexander Pushkin

Tatiana falls in love with Eugene Onegin but she's like a white trash country girl and he's fabulous and hobnobs with the rich and famous and wants to have fun all the time. He keeps rejecting her and embarrassing her. Years later he runs into her to find that she's become absolutely *fabulous*.... but married. He tries to persuade her to leave her husband but she won't do it. She ruins his life by not being a slut.

Lesson: If you don't become a slut, you'll ruin a man's life. If you ruin a man's life, you're a slut.

5) *The Idiot* by Fyodor Dostoyevsky

That dirty whore Nastassya is torn between nice guy Myshkin and passionate bad boy Rogozhin. She almost marries the nice guy but runs away with the passionate bad boy at the last minute, who ends up stabbing her to death. Oops! Wrong choice.

Lesson: Women who have freedom to choose get stabbed to death.

6) *Swan Lake* by Tchaikovsky

> A good swan with a spell cast on her falls
> in love with a dude. A black swan ruins
> everything and the dude and the good
> swan get to be together, but they also
> have to die.

> Lesson: Good girls finish last.

7) *Uncle Vanya* by Anton Chekhov

> Sonia helps her uncle run her father's
> estate and is in love with the town
> Doctor. But Sonia is plain and the
> doctor's affection is directed at a striking
> new visitor who Sonia can't compete
> with looks-wise. She resigns herself to
> doing paperwork in a chair for the rest of
> her life and prays she'll find solace and
> rest after her death.

> Lesson: Plain girls don't get shit.

8) *Doctor Zhivago* by Boris Pasternak

> A lot of confusing shit happens. Yuri and
> Lara have to leave Moscow. Yuri comes
> back first, has children with another
> woman, and dies. Lara comes back
> looking for him, ends up going to his
> funeral, and Stalin sends her to the Gulag
> where she dies.

Lesson: Curiosity killed the cat (woman).

WHEN SHIT GETS REAL

1) Joseph Stalin's 2nd wife

Joseph's Stalin's second wife Nadezhda Sergeevna Alliluyeva suffered from mood swings and hysteria (which had nothing to do with her being married to a ruthless, murderous dictator). They fought a lot, which was obviously all her fault. After a public fight one night, she shot herself to death. That detail was buried and it was announced as an unfortunate death due to "appendicitis."

Lesson: You don't have to be a slut to die violently and prematurely. You just have to be a woman.

2) Catherine The Great

Catherine The Great had sex with over 20 men (always younger) throughout her life. She seems to be the only person in Russian history who liked to have fun. So of course, men tarnished her name by spreading a rumor that she died while fucking a horse.

Lesson: Don't let anyone know you're having fun (if you're a woman). This is where the blank expression you've been practicing comes in handy.

3) The first wife of Ivan the Terrible

Throughout his life, Ivan the Terrible graced eight women with his violence, rage, and paranoia. What a giver! He picked his first wife, Anastasia, out of 1500 brides. He was like the original "Bachelor!" He is rumored to have loved her with all his heart. Despite that, he made her bear six children. She was poisoned by the Russian nobles who hated Ivan. He executed them.

Lesson: Expect to pay for your husband's mistakes.

4) The second wife of Ivan the Terrible

Maria Temryukovna was Muslim and Ivan grew to hate her. Boy, they could have used that Muslim ban back then! After a bunch of people decided she was a witch, he went ahead and poisoned her to death. Even though the Russian nobles had nothing to do with it this time, he executed them anyway for good measure.

Lesson: Avoid being born Muslim or else you'll pay for your sins, you pagan demon!

5) The third wife of Ivan the Terrible

Now a widower two times over, Ivan reluctantly went back on ABC and asked Chris Harrison for help finding him a new bride. This time, he chose Marfa Sobakina out of only 12 finalists. She immediately started exhibiting signs of being poisoned. At this point, Ivan should have maybe checked his medicine cabinet to see what was in there. Anyway, she died. Ivan went nuts and executed a bunch more people, including his second wife's brother. Side note: He claimed this marriage was never consummated.

Lesson: Be a slut on your wedding night or you'll die.

6) The fourth wife of Ivan the Terrible

It would have been illegal for Ivan to get married a fourth time, but since his first marriage was never legit, he was aight. He married Anna Koltovskaya without the church's OK, but she was infertile. Since he only had six kids and needed loads more, she was useless to him and he imprisoned her in a convent.

Lesson: Women have two choices. They can be fertile, or they can become nuns.

7) The fifth wife of Ivan the Terrible

Anna Vasilchikova was another wife that the church did not approve of. Chris Harrison was really not coming through for Ivan, as he got fed up with her after two years and also sent her to prison (the convent). To one-up himself from his last wife, he upped the ante and had Anna killed in captivity.

Lesson: Dude. Don't marry Ivan the Terrible.

8) The sixth wife of Ivan the Terrible

The bad luck train continues! Vasilisa Melentyeva was also a widow, so you'd think she and Ivan would have a lot in common. Alas, no. Shortly after she and Ivan wed, she jumped into bed with a hot prince for some steamy sex. They weren't using their heads, so Ivan had his cut off and sent Vasilisa to a convent. Geez, he's become the talent booker of this convent by now! She died there of "mysterious causes."

Lesson: See "The fourth wife of Ivan the Terrible."

9) The seventh wife of Ivan the Terrible

Maria Dolgorukaya must have never read a newspaper, because she became the seventh wife of Ivan. She also took a lover, thus proving to history that maybe Ivan was really bad in bed. The network behind "The Bachelor" told him to change things up this time, so instead of his usual "unexplained death at convent" trope, he had Maria drowned.

Lesson: Learn how to swim (if you're a woman).

10) The eighth wife of Ivan the Terrible

Eight is great! Ivan married Maria Nagaya, who bore him one son. He was fifty-one years old at this point; quite a productive man! He finally died and Maria and her son went into exile. Seven years later, her son died "under mysterious circumstances." She was then forced to pretend another dude was her son so that he could become Tsar. That phony was killed by an angry mob a year later because he engaged in an interfaith marriage. Like father, like fake son!

Lesson: Don't be born a woman.

MINORITIES

Interracial marriage is looked down upon. Black, Hispanic and Asian people are going to have to stick to their own kind....while getting deported.

LGBTQ

Being gay is basically illegal. Gay people are going to have to marry hetero if they want to survive.

MILLENNIALS

Millennials are going to have a harder time than anyone, as they do not know how to interact with authority.

BONUS TIP

What goes better with black bread than a black eye? Get all your girlfriends together, get dressed up, and show off your domestic abuse bruises in a Russian version of "Who Took It Best?"

Chapter 5: Family relations

Prepare for multigenerational cohabitation since we are all going to be poor and living in communal housing. Having dirt on your own family is crucial, as you may be competing with your siblings and cousins for the composting scraps which will comprise your meals.

THE HIERARCHY OF RUSSIAN FAMILY LOYALTY

Putin
Husband
Dentist (you use his office at night for secret meetings)
Mother
Your cat
Father
Grandmother
Your dog
Grandfather
Wife

RUSSIAN MYTHS

Looking over your shoulder every time you leave your apartment is not enough. Russians see potential for conspiracy and collusion in everything. If you don't learn how to maneuver by the beacons of myths and superstitions you may as well wrap yourself in a Hillary banner and don a Pussy Power hat. It doesn't matter if you're eating an open face caviar sandwich while on your Bluetooth. Fail to abide by these myths and superstitions and you will be the first in your family to disappear.

"You'll get a sore throat if you drink cold water."

"You'll get the flu if you don't wear a hat, even in the summer."

"You'll get pneumonia if you don't wear slippers."

"You'll get a sinus infection if you go outside with wet hair."

"You'll get a cold in your vagina if you sit on the floor." You actually will be sitting on the floor because you had to burn your sofa and dining chairs to generate enough heat to survive the winter. But you will not get a cold in your vagina. You may, however, die of boredom.

RUSSIAN SUPERSTITIONS

Superstitions are a great way to keep people in a low grade, permanent discomfort. Blend in by abiding by any and all of the below.

You're supposed to sit in silence for a minute before traveling. This is the only time when everyone is obligated to sit in silence, and not audibly insult and judge each other (yet, still secretly disgusted and suspicious of each other).

Never kiss hello or goodbye over a threshold in a doorway. A threshold divides people, and Russia wants to unite the entire world (as long as the entire world abides by Russia's rules).

When you sneeze it's considered a confirmation of your latest thought or statement. For example, if someone tells you "You look tired" and then you sneeze it means that you'll look tired for the rest of your life.

GROWING PAINS

You will have literal pain growing up because Russians will begin molding you into a useful family asset from your early years. This may include torture prep and sleeping on a hard surface, probably the floor, because all of the other sleeping areas - even the kitchen cot - are occupied by elders and extended family. Plus Russians live and die by the rule that it is "good for your back" to sleep on a piece of plywood.

RUSSIAN FAMILY RULES

- You may never have a babysitter; no intelligent Russian family would pay a stranger to potentially spy on them. Instead you will be raised by your grandparents and you'll learn about the golden age of American culture from soap operas and sitcoms (and romance novels). Your grandmother may also be watching closely to learn how to make "I'm not a spy" faces, and how to look up dramatically into the distance after she has an "aha" moment out in the field.

- If you have a pet cat or dog you must name him after a famous Russian poet or intellectual, and declare that the animal has taken on the artistic and/or depressive temperament of an artist not appreciated until after his time. This is important in order to fit in, but also the pet is a key player in the ecosystem, sauntering out when surprise visitors or neighbors show up and disarming them with their depressive charm.

- All children must to learn play the piano, learn how to draw a still-life or portrait in perspective and do their times tables before they're five. These skills will come in handy in the labor camps where they can play concerts for top officials and use their math skills to calculate how to dig their Shawshank Redemption hole out of there (into a better labor camp in the neighboring town).

- If you really want to impress the new regime, who have eyes everywhere, send your kid to school with an open face caviar sandwich with sardines on the side, sliced cucumbers and pickled watermelon. If the other kids at school tease them, go to the school and punch those kids in the face and tell them they'd better get used it. We are going to be eating mostly cured and canned goods in the near future when all of our trade agreements vanish and we are stuck with imports from only one country.

- Stand over your children while they do their homework. If they say they're done, tell them they're liars, their teachers are idiots, their handwriting is terrible, and drag them back to school to demand more homework – especially over summer vacation - so your child isn't as stupid as these idiots. It's the least you can do to help your kids thrive despite the changes in our education system. You've got to take matters in your own hands!

- Have an affectionate, yet mean – loving, yet insulting – nickname for your child.

For example: "My stupidfatlittlegirlishka." "My idiotgaygoodfornothingsonishka." This will make your children strive to do better so that their nickname will improve to "my aboveaveragedaughtershka."

- If your parents try to force you to eat random nightshade vegetables for breakfast, tell them you want to have orange juice and cereal while they're still available in the country.

- If your mom gets mad at you, buy her a fur. She'll forgive you...until you come home with a Jewish boyfriend. Then you'll be in debt to her for a diamond choker, which hopefully the boyfriend can get if Jews are still allowed to dominate the jewelry market.

- If your parents ask you what you want to be, they're actually testing you. No matter what you want to be, you're going to be a computer scientist, computer programmer, or computer salesman. Anything with "computer" in the title will keep them at bay. Be smart and answer correctly.

- Apply to several out of state colleges even though you will ultimately end up attending a college no more than five miles away from home and living in your parents house. If you attempt to live in the dorms this will be the only topic of conversation at every family gathering until they wear you down and realize it's just easier to live at home. If you do make it out of the house into the dorms (three houses down), expect your mother to deliver hot food to you daily and still do your laundry, brush your hair, and kidnap you back to living at home. It will all work out, because the dorms are going to be converted to jail cells.

RUSSIAN GRANDPARENTS

Respecting the elderly is a top priority in Russian culture. Grandparents are the holy grail of the hierarchy. They also make the best spies. And cakes.

Make sure your grandmother stops dying her hair, wears thick reading glasses, forgets to put her dentures on, and walks hunched over with a cane. She must appear almost completely ancient, hard of hearing, and nearly blind, when she is really very spry and bright. Ideally she is a trained master magician with sleight of hand that will allow her to steal from strangers while carefully planting bugs in their pockets and purses. You'll probably want to keep an eye on her in case the government notices her undercover skills and kidnaps her, likely for their spy-in-training regime.

Grandma's daily rounds to the pharmacy, the bazaar, and past the newsstand will double as an environmental scan to scope out suspicious activity so you know where your enemies are meeting and which streets and corners to avoid on the way to work (if you're the recommended non-political type). Spying devices can also be planted into gold teeth, glasses and dentures. This is one of the reasons that grandma is such an excellent puppet for the cause.

Because police rarely bother the elderly, she's the perfect mule to deliver and retrieve banned literature, music, and Meryl Streep movies to and from secret locations. Make sure that no visit to the market for a bunch of beats or buckwheat groats goes to waste: she should always be stashing something in those grains. Your uncle's friend from pioneer camp is closely connected to the guy who delivers the early morning produce, and he will help you to coordinate these exchanges. In return for his assistance you will offer up your grandmother's services as spy to him as needed.

Hair can hide a lot of things. Many American women lose hair as they get older. A Russian woman's hair actually gets bigger and bigger. It's a natural phenomenon and why wigs made of

Russian hair are some of the most expensive in the world. It gets so thick, you can transport cans, laptops, notebooks and paper towels in your grandmother's hairdo. Urban legend has it that a Russian grandmother actually won WWII by kidnapping Hitler in her bouffant. When using your grandmother as a "Moscow mule," make sure everything is evenly weighted or else she'll fall over. In Russia, the elderly know all about "I've fallen and can't get up." But they have no system to actually help them get back up. Once your grandmother has fallen in the street and the contraband spills out of her hair, not only is she done for, but people will take the supplies and keep walking. However, this is considered an honorable cause of death. Plus, you'll have an extra cot in your apartment now.

While your grandmother is hitting the streets doing recon, your grandfather is back at home napping while the grandchildren are pickpocketing him.

STAYING "CONNECTED"

Russians love nothing more that to make connections to advance their position in life, get a good deal on products and services, and be introduced to "interesting" people, by which we mean people who make more money and will serve gourmet food and top-shelf liquor at dinner parties (plus, bring the fattest envelope when it's *your* party). Bonus points are awarded if said people can get them a deal on something (TV, cell phone) or introduce their children to someone they should marry (for money).

Russians love to play matchmaker and then remind you how grateful you should be to them for setting your son up with their co-worker's niece, even though they're not really happy together. But, at least they were matched up and now you owe your friend a favor! And, they're off the market for gossip about "why are they still single." This is far worse than tolerating a boring and loveless relationship. Just give them some time and soon they'll make the most of each other's connections, and hopefully produce some grandchildren.

Remember Russian UPS? This is also a product of making connections.   Before someone becomes your enemy you should analyze what they are capable of doing for you. Even if they're mostly useless, they could at least deliver something to your sister's former classmate's son on their next trip.

HOW TO BE A SON OR DAUGHTER

Children are expected to play along with everything that is asked of them. The biggest difference between daughters and sons is that daughters are expected to show up everywhere early, wear make-up, look fertile and help set the table and then clean-up. Sons are just expected to show up, usually late. At least they showed up! They'll be happy you came at all.

Whether a boy or a girl, to survive you must be the sibling who makes the better toasts and accompanies your parents to all their doctor appointments.

HOW TO BE A GRANDCHILD

Report on what really goes on with your parents and you will be rewarded with extra Napoleon cake (and cognac - shhh). This is a great way to sharpen your spy game.

HOW TO BE A MOTHER

Your main job is to make everybody suffer and come back for more. By torturing your children from a young age you are actually doing them a great service, preparing them for the mental torment they will soon encounter at the labor camps.

A Russian mother's greatest skill is the ability to ask a million questions about absolutely nothing of consequence. Did you eat? What did you eat? Did you heat it up? Did you put it on a plate? Do you have forks? Are you warm enough? Is your heat on? Do you need a blanket? These questions apply well into your thirties and beyond. The good news is that you will develop an immunity to this never ending line of questioning and will quickly learn how to maneuver cross-examinations in your favor. A great way to distract a Russian mother is to tell her that you're hungry. These words are like a narc dog discovering a kilo of heroin on a raid.

HOW TO BE A FATHER

The harder they cry, the more they learn. This includes your wife — domestic violence is basically encouraged now! As the father you must look authoritarian and intimidating until you make someone cry. Then, once they are in tears, grab your guitar and play them a famous Russian folk song while smoking a cigarette and doing shots of vodka. This will perpetuate the unhealthy cycle of punishment and reward. Again, this is all training for later in life when your children are being tortured in exile. Except, when they burst into tears in Siberia there will be no guitar and no music. They will return from exile hardened and ready to help out with the family business!

HEROES AND ROLE MODELS

Unlike the clean cut inspirational American heroes that you are used to, like Pocahontas, Eleanor Roosevelt, Winnie the Pooh, and Barack

Obama you must completely redefine this list and expectations. From now on you will draw your strength from tyrannical and controversial figures such as Ivan the Terrible, Ursula from The Little Mermaid, and Andrew Jackson. Why? They are examples of the kind of strength, strong-arming, and savvy discrimination that is required to survive in this new land.

Your wife's not cooperating or going along with the program? Chop her head off. She won't have much to say after that. Hire minorities but don't pay them a cent. They should just be grateful they have somewhere to go and a few scraps to eat and a nice place to hang out. If the authorities question why you're employing minorities calmly explain that they're helping you build a wall to keep themselves out of your yard.

Bonus Tip:

To score extra points with your parents, copy-edit their complaint and mail-in rebate emails for them. Aim for three complaints per day to various vendors like the local grocer and pharmacist about their terrible experiences and subpar service. Freebies are worth more than your love!

Chapter 6: Bullying your way to success

Russian people might have any and all of these careers in their lifespans:

Doctor
Dentist/hygienist*
Herbalife salesperson
Manicurist
Cab driver
Prostitute
Internet troll
Engineer
Piano teacher
Something with computers
Russian restaurant owner
Aesthetician
Mathematician
Gymnast
Model
Attorney
Oligarch
Ballerina
Translator for the mafia
Mail-order bride
Scientist
Poet
Coder
A student at the KGB Academy
*The dentist and hygienist are usually related to each other.

Unacceptable careers:
Helping minorities or working at a job as a minority.

CAREERS: A CLOSER LOOK

Doctor
You'll treat people during the day and help the sick, yada yada yada, but nighttime is the right time for a doctor. This is when your office is used for secret meetings. Revolutions have been known to start in stirrups.

Dentist/Hygienist
Russians don't have the best teeth, due to having to eat rocks, so you've got job security until the end of time. Secret meetings also happen here. If someone doesn't agree with your plan to overthrow the government, just squirt some laughing gas into their mouth, then make them sign the petition.

Herbalife salesperson
Starvation and binge eating can keep a person's weight up, and that's where you come in. The Herbalife diet is sure to ensure a person continues yo-yoing for life, thus always coming back to you for more diet help.

Manicurist
You file people's nails and taxes. Why not make an extra buck?

Cab driver
This is one of the most popular careers for Russian men. Anyone can be a cab driver. In autocratic anarchy, there are no rules. If you're driving home from work and see someone

hailing a cab, just pull over and quote them something ridiculous. This is completely normal. People will get into the first car that pulls over. It's a great way to swindle your way into extra pocket money. Russians invented Uber but never get any credit, which is why they hacked our election.

Prostitute
This is the second most sought after career for a Russian woman, after model. The police usually take care of bookings and payments. All you have to do is show up in 11-inch stilettos with bleached blond hair and a live animal around your neck.

Internet troll
Your job is to spread fake news under fake identities. The first person who'll retweet you is POTUS.

Engineer
Given your skillset, you'll probably be moved to a remote location to work next to a lab in an unmarked government building.

Piano teacher
The secret police have wire tapps in your microwave because you have a constant stream of new people in your home. It's cool, you know about it.

Something with computers
Hacker.

Russian restaurant owner
You're like Artie Bucco from The Sopranos. A lot of bad people doing bad shit eat nightly at your establishment, but you can't say anything because they tip well and also they'd kill you.

Aesthetician
You'll be gainfully employed, since Russian women can't show any signs of aging, otherwise they deserve the punches they have coming to them. Also you'll be an asset to the officials by storing vials of poison marked "anti-wrinkle serum."

Mathematician
Russians are great at math, so there will be a lot of competition for math jobs. There are more Russian mathematicians than Russian mathematician jobs. You do the math.

Gymnast
You have to do extra splits when the President comes to watch your routine. In bed.

Model
Great career for failed strippers and women not quite ready to be prostitutes and anyone looking for a rich older man.

Attorney
Basically you'll be approached by everyone in your family, and all of your parents' friends for free legal advice about how to sue for a car accident (even though it was their fault) and/or because the cashier at Home Depot may or may not have whispered "Russian spy" under their breath during a recent transaction.

Oligarch
You run the banks, the government, hospitals, churches, media and the oil, water and food supply. You go on a lot of vacations.

Ballerina
You have to dance like EVERYBODY'S watching. Because they are, they'll point out your flaws if you make any mistakes and you'll be fired from the ballet company for humiliating them.

Translator for the mafia
You already know too much just reading this job description.

Mail-order bride
As Russia slowly but surely grows its empire, there will soon be nowhere to send mail-order brides. This soon-to-be-antiquated profession was great while it lasted, especially for gymnasts who could keep their bodies in a tight ball for hours inside those FedEx boxes. However, old

printed catalogues can be burned for heat and fuel.

Scientist
You'll be working in a lab in an unmarked government building next to the engineers. If you mention climate change or clean air, you won't be fed. Focus on nuclear, oil, and big pharma.

Poet
The most tragic, yet most celebrated, yet least rewarded of the Russian professions, the poet mostly works on a park bench, a pile of papers in his windowless apartment, or on a cement block in prison.

Coder
You illegally stream TV shows, help hackers influence elections, and assist the government in breaking into journalists' home computers.

A Student at the KGB Academy
The most lucrative KGB agents seem to work as double or triple agents. If you get paid twice by one government and once by another, you may have enough money to bribe your closest loved ones out of their internment camps.

WORKPLACE RULES

Negotiating is an art created by and perfected by Russians. You won't believe how much your life will improve once you learn how to complain and identify a bad deal when it's being handed to you so you can say "NYET!" No longer will bad hombres stand a chance at stealing a good opportunity right from under your nose. The same goes for those entitled millennials.

At work it's important to remember that your employer is lucky to have you, even if they don't appreciate you and stuck you in the cubicle next to the woman who is always crying about her son in the army. Make sure you remind your husband/wife/children daily, as you're taking out the trash/cooking dinner/leaving for work/taking a shower/filing your nails, that you're making the biggest sacrifices for the fewest rewards.

There will no longer be a thing called HR. Instead most offices will have a new umbrella category that will include the formerly known Operations, Marketing & Public Relations departments. The new department will just be called "SOVIET": Surveillance Ordinance Vehemence Injustice Effacement & Tyranny. They are also in charge of payroll and vacation requests. You'll be getting paid in potatoes and rubles and your vacations will be spent at the company's farmland harvesting the crops.

Alternative vacation requests must be supported by proof that you will be visiting labor camps or going on a tour of Putin's favorite landmarks.

While you are working hard to keep the job you hate while flirting with your superiors, your boss may barely be lifting a finger except to sexually harass you. This falls in the category of legal behavior along with the decriminalization of domestic violence. In fact, you should consider yourself lucky; if your boss is flirting with you, it means job security for at least three months! You're even luckier if your boss flirts with you but your husband doesn't beat you. You will be the envy of all of your friends, even though your husband is unemployed and sleeps all day.

FREEBIES AND PERKS

You should always be disgusted by a first offer, whether at a restaurant or at the DMV. If you're going out to eat, send the food back, reject the wine, and threaten to walk out. Make sure you're wearing a diamond choker. Do not agree to eat there again until they've sent you a complimentary bottle of vodka and platter of smoked fish. This will earn you respect because it shows you know how to negotiate.

At the DMV, even if you get the first appointment, complain about the time being too early, even though you won't need to wait in line. Actually, say goodbye to "lines." There are no lines in Russia. There are anarchist mobs that gather mass very quickly and have caused stampedes, injuries and deaths. They are perfectly legal. It is totally acceptable to walk over a mob as it forms, stepping on knees, elbows, shoulders and heads, to get to the other side and get your new driver's license. We call this survival of the fittest.

HOW TO GET OUT OF PAYING PARKING TICKETS

If you're a woman, show up at your local precinct with deep cleavage, a lot of jewelry, full makeup, and a box of Russian candies that are named after forest animals, like the bow-legged bear, the fuzzy squirrel and the birds nest. Then, let them nest their eyes on you.

If you are a man, you are always right. Repeat: "I am always right." It doesn't matter what you said, did, carried, smuggled, or stole: you were right.

Survival Tips:

- Always carry cash in your pocket to bribe cops.

- When negotiating for a car, stand up and leave if you don't like the asking price.

- Come to your condo board meetings and complain loudly in Russian without offering any solutions. And then leave.

- Blackmail people with information you have about them and tell them you have someone who can crack that cell phone.

- Don't pay medical bills.

- Steal free, sell high.

- Always negotiate. Even when someone gives you what you want, for the price you want, call them a stupid idiot. For example, "That idiot gave me exactly what I asked for."

Bonus tip:

Casual ways to suggest a bribe:

Innocently say "Oh, is that a $20 bill on the ground?" and saunter away.

Ask "Is that real leather?" as you put your hand in the military wife's purse and hope your hand comes back up with cold hard cash.

"I wasn't speeding, officer. I recorded it on this brand new iPhone. You'll see for yourself when you replay the video at home."

"I'm pretty sure my appointment is now and not in three hours. Why don't you check one more time using this gold watch?"

Chapter 7: Language

Now that you've mastered your new way of life, it's time to adjust your language. This chapter will provide key phrases, vocabulary, slang, and outdated proverbs that are back in style.

RUSSIFIED HASHTAGS

#FiringSquadGoals
#PrisonSelfie
#CrimeaRiver
#5YearPrisonBodyTransformation
#MoscowDrugMule
#DreadSquare
#Syr-iously
#SundayGunday
#FBF #FlashBackFascism
#RatsofInstagram
#IWillTotesalitarianismBeThere
#DamnAutocorrectacy
#SpiesOfInstagram
#InstaFollowLiterallyGuysImBeingFollowedomg
#FaceCrookLive
#FaceCrime
#UKraiGirl

PROVERBS

Now that you've mastered the art of gossip the next thing you must do is to quote some Russian proverbs. Be sure to throw in at least one proverb in the course of any conversation, whether you're talking to a head of state or the mailman. Here are some handy lines to keep people from asking too many questions about where you're *really* from. Don't ask what they mean - or else everyone will know you're not really Russian. You don't want to be a laughingstock, in a prison cell.

- Love is cruel. You'll fall in love with a goat.

- Love isn't a potato. You can't throw it out the window.

- The appetite will come with eating.

- Without torture, no science.

- Flattery makes friends and truth makes enemies.

- There is no way for two deaths to come to you, but from one you will never run away.

- The cat knows whose meat it has eaten.

- If you could know where you fall, you would spread some straw.

- He beats you because he really loves you (but only once a year).

For centuries artists have created new and interesting work out of despair. Be sure to mix in some new proverbs daily to remind yourself and others that nobody is looking out for us.

- A frown is just a smile, pointed towards hell.

- Hope is a four letter word.

- When life gives you lemons, give up.

- When you run out of reasons to live, start making a list of reasons to die. That should keep you busy until old age.

- You should always dream, at night. During the day, there's no room for dreaming. Stop being an idiot.

- Women who tell the truth have nothing to hide. Men who tell the truth are stupid.

- If your enemy surprises you from behind, make the most of it.

- When all hope of love is lost, it's time to look in the mirror and understand you waited too long, you stupid idiot.

- When facing hard times, do *not* keep your head up. You won't see your enemies trying to trip you.

- If you meet a man who knows exactly what he's doing, then you should be very, very suspicious.

- Keep your friends closer than your enemies. They'll let you use them as a human shield if need be.

- A marriage is like a duel. Only one person survives. That person is the one who committed murder.

- To love is to despise with great relish. They are lucky you feel anything at all.

- Children are a reflection of their parents. So don't look them in the eye.

- If you start your day with a cold shower you won't end up in a cold grave.

- "No" mean "yes," and "yes" means you should ask for more.

TRANSLATIONS

SAYING	TRANSLATION
Bleen	Pancake (also a euphemism for the more offensive "blyad").
Blyad	Whore
Palnoy durdom	Total madhouse
Ty papraveelas	You got fat
Ty ochen pahudela	You're too thin
Nye kamu nye gavaree…potomu chto ya skaju	Don't tell anyone this gossip…because that's my job
Vyhadee zamusz uzhe	Take a husband already!
Kak babushka pashyvayet?	How's your grandmother
Kak davleniye?	How's your blood pressure?
Skeedkee v Stop n Shopye	There's a sale at Stop N' Shop
Durak	Idiot (male)
Dura	Idiot (female)
Dosveedanya, semya!	Goodbye, family! (As you're getting arrested).
Priviet	Type of Vodka or "hi"
Starosts nye radasts	Old age is not happiness
Vozmi syebya v ruki	Get a grip

Russify your name

The final step to becoming Russian is to take on a new name. Depending on your last name, you'll likely add a "sky," "ov," "vich," "shkin," "ev," "ka," "yov," "khin," or "glov."

Don't be precious about your first name. Just make it Svetlana, Natasha, Boris or Dimitry.

OLD AMERICAN NAME	NEW RUSSIAN NAME
Molly Jones	Svetlana Jonesky
Colleen Cunningham	Natasha Cunninghamovich
Jon Lewis	Boris Lewisky
Kevin Clark	Dimitry Clarkin
Meryl Streep	Over-rated
Hillary Clinton	Life in prison
Helen Taylor	Natasha Taylorova
Carlos Rodriguez	Dimitry Rodrigovich
Susan Devito	Svetlana Devityova
Ari Cohen	Jew
Susan Sarandon	Enemy of the state
Jimmy Miller	Boris Millershkin
Min Chen	Svetlana Chenova
Blue Ivy Carter	Natasha Carterskaya
Oprah	Svetlana
Barack Obama	Boris Obamka
Bruce Willis	Bruce Willis!

Bonus Tip:

Learn to tell the difference between "beet" and "beat."
"I'll have the beet soup today."
"I try not to beat my wife on Sundays"

Chapter 8: Games and entertainment

Games like cards, charades, trivia and quizzes are huge in Russian culture. You'll need something to help you pass the time at home when there are no jobs and nothing to eat.

1) **Playing "I Spy" with your kids.**

Playing I Spy with your kids is just like it used to be, except now you'll be writing down everything they notice and sending those documents to the government. Every year of their lives you will gradually bring in more relevant sightings. For example, when they're toddlers it will be something like "I spy an airplane!" A few years later that will turn into: "I spy a missile!" By the time they're graduating from high school it will turn into, "Abort mission or deploy back-up."

2) **Finish the Putin quote....**

I don't read books by people who have betrayed the Motherland. **I just read their obituaries.**

Those who fight corruption should be clean themselves. **That's why I don't fight corruption.**

Spying has always gone on since ancient times. We are just celebrating tradition. **What's America's problem?**

Protest actions and propaganda are two slightly different things. **But both are illegal unless I authorize them.**

It's alarming that military intervention in internal conflicts in foreign countries has become commonplace for the United States. **That's Russia's job.**

If the nation is not capable of preserving itself and reproducing, if it loses its vital bearings and ideals, then it doesn't need foreign enemies - it will fall apart on its own. **Like America, any day now! High fives all around!**

I am convinced that the norm in Russia should become a family with three children. **So that we can overpopulate and conquer the rest of the world, starting with Ukraine and ending with Canada.**

3) Russian Mad Libs - Comrade Libs

My grandmother went to the _____ because there was a sale on _____. When she got there, she couldn't find the _____. She asked to speak to the _____. He told her to go _____ herself. She _____ him across the _____ and said "I have buried two _____ and lived under _____-cracy until I was 75. Now I'm living under it again. Don't tell me what to _____. I'll ask you again. Where is the _____ that's on sale?" Ten minutes later, she was walking home with 20 pounds of _____. Unfortunately, she got robbed so we ended up skipping dinner.

After my arrest, I was put in a _____. I couldn't see or hear anything because they put a _____ over my _____. After a few days, I met _____. _____ offered me some _____ in exchange for my gold tooth. The _____ he/she gave me ended up being broken. I spent _____ years trying to prove my _____ but there is no court of _____ and no laws to protect people like me in search of _____. Thank you for listening to my _____ request. I promise to be a _____ citizen and do my duty as a _____. Humbly yours, _____-tsov.

My cousins and I hacked the American _____. It was super easy. First, we gained access to the Democratic _____. Then we released all the _____ we found to _____ who's currently living in exile in _____. He happens to hate _____. Then, we spread _____ news on social media sites like _____, _____ and _____. The idiotic _____ bought it. On _____ day, we rigged the voting _____ by contacting _____. We kept President _____ aware of all of our moves via _____. He was grateful. He sent us a _____ to show his appreciation. God bless USA!

At my aunt's _____ party, my _____
pulled me aside to discuss the _____ deal
and the transfer of _____ happening at
midnight. Then, the waiters came out with
_____ so we ate. When we were finally full,
it was time for more _____. I got in a
fight with _____ and he/she knocked a tooth
out. Luckily, my _____ who lives with us is
a dental surgeon. Meanwhile, my mother was spying
on everyone with a hidden _____ in her
_____. She likes to report back on who has
gotten the _____-est. My _____ got
arrested and then my other _____ went
missing. All in all, it was a great party.

4) True or False

Find really ridiculous news stories and mix them
together with fake stories and see who can guess
which is true of false!

True or False?

A Russian woman gets attacked by a wolf and ends
up killing the wolf.

Man shot in the neck with an arrow survives.

Naked Russian woman holds her breath for 10
minutes underwater to swim with – and tame - two
white whales.

Russia places American President in power.

White Supremacist appointed to NSA 150 years after slavery abolished and 50 years after segregation is abolished.

President with Jewish grandchildren appoints a Nazi to the NSA.

Answer key: They're all true.

5) Slut shame your neighbor

Have your neighbor's locks changed while she's out having a one-night stand and then make her stand in the hallway with last night's clothing on for nine-and-a-half weeks.

6) Drink To The Death

So simple. Sit down with an enemy, two shot glasses and a bottle of vodka. Start drinking at the same time. Somewhere in the middle of the game, kill him.

7) Win, Lose, or Die

You'll be playing this daily on the streets, by living your life.

8) Wait, Wait...Don't Kill Me!

Actually, just kill me.

9) Who Wants To Be a Prisoner?

Your uncle on the cot has spotted the secret police crossing the street and coming towards your door. All 19 of you stand in a circle and play rock/paper/scissors shoot until one person is left standing. He's the one who gets arrested today. Don't worry, everyone will have their turn.

10) The Newly-Deported Game!

Divide your friends into two sections of your bedroom and draw a red line in between you. Pick the brownest-looking one of all of you and try to push him over red line as he struggles. The people on the other side will try to push him back towards you since they can't take anymore people either. Do this until he screams out his safe word. Then start again with the second most brown-looking person in the friend group.

11) Press Your Luck

Gather all of your family and friends in one place and see how many insults you can throw out at each other until a serious fight breaks out.

12) Russian Hang-Man

Find a traitor and hang him.

TV

There's going to be one TV channel now, run by the government. No need to worry! You can still catch all of your favorite shows. They'll just have a new spin to them.

1) You're in Jeopardy

Real people compete through the streets of Moscow in a high speed car chase. The KGB chases them all the way to the border where they get arrested. There are no follow up interviews.

2) The Price is Too High

Middle-class people try to go shopping but can't find anything they can afford.

3) Fear Factor

A live-streamed webcam image of the Red Square.

4) The Hunger Games

24 children are given bows and arrows and thrown into the forest to hunt. It's live streamed on the steps of the Lincoln Memorial. Nobody survives.

5) Who's Country Is It, Anyway?

People are pitted against each other to see who's more patriotic. Most episodes have a false finish when the audience finds out a gay person has won. That gay person is sent down through a trapdoor on the floor, never to be heard from again, and the prize is always given to the big, white, Russian man in tinted glasses who's half asleep for the whole hour.

6) Supermarket Bleak

Families have 10 rubles to spend in an empty supermarket. They must buy 10 rubles worth of products, yet the shelves are completely empty. It's a little boring but there's nothing else on, so….

7) Survivor

Contestants emulate Russian dissidents like Nikolai Gorokhov, who "fell" out of his fourth floor window while "moving a bathtub" and "survived."

8) Double Dare (you to be a Democrat)

I mean you can try, but good luck getting anything done! Actually, same is true for trying to be a Republican.

9) High Rollers of Congress

The old C-Span.

10) To Tell the Truth You Don't Have to Be President

A live telecast of all of the President's speeches.

11) The Weakest Link

Any member of the parliament.

Bonus Tip:
It's all fun and games until somebody loses an eye. JK. There's a famous Russian schoolyard game where eyes are often lost and it's NBD. Ages 6+.

Chapter 9: Say "Dosveedanya" to your rights!

Now that you know how to say goodbye in Russian, go ahead and say it out loud....to your rights!

What you're losing:

Freedom of speech
Freedom of press
Freedom to not be hit by your spouse
Freedom to protest
Freedom to be gay
Amongst many, many, many, many others

What you're gaining:

Weight. From all the starch you're eating.
Here are some examples of what happens when people try to exercise these freedoms. Enjoy!

Freedom of Speech

Boris Nemstov, a high profile anti-Putin Russian opposition leader, dedicated two decades of his life to protesting the autocracy and resisting the government. In an interview, he said "I love Russia and want the best for her, so for me criticizing Putin is a very patriotic activity because these people are leading Russia to ruin. Everybody who supports them in fact supports a regime that is destroying the country, and so they are the ones who hate Russia. And those who criticize this regime, those who fight against it, they are the patriots."

He was shot dead on a bridge near The Kremlin in early 2015. Putin said he would lead the investigation himself. No arrests have been made.

Nikolai Gorokhov, a lawyer for a late Russian whistleblower's family, was due to appear in court on Wednesday March 22nd and represent the deceased's mother. Unfortunately, he "fell" out of his four story building the night before his scheduled court date. Russian state run media reported that he "accidentally fell while moving a bathtub."

The message: Never, ever question authority while taking a bath.

Freedom of Press

Every year, the government will try to silence journalists. Fun times!

Russian journalist and activist Anna Politkovskaya was fiercely opposed to the Chechnyan war and to Vladimir Putin.

She wrote "We are hurtling back into a Soviet abyss, into an information vacuum that spells death from our own ignorance. All we have left is the internet, where information is still freely available. For the rest, if you want to go on working as a journalist, it's total servility to Putin. Otherwise, it can be death, the bullet, poison, or trial—whatever our special services, Putin's guard dogs, see fit."

She was murdered in her apartment building in 2006.

Khadzhimurad Kamalov was the founder of the Dagestan weekly newspaper Chernovik. He investigated and covered police abuse, Islamic extremism, and corruption. During difficult financial times he put up his own apartment as collateral to keep the paper going. He was shot to death fourteen times outside of his office in 2011. He was among six journalists killed that year.

There are dozens more stories like this. They're all probably one big coincidence.

The message: By all means, be a reporter. But please don't report on the truth.

Freedom to not be hit

Russia's domestic violence problem has reached atomic levels. Russian parliament took the first steps to decriminalize domestic violence in early 2017 by making it legal to beat your spouse once a year. But domestic abuse has been an issue plaguing Russia for years prior to that. According to the Russian Interior Ministry, there were four million cases of reported domestic violence in 2015. There could be just as many unreported cases. We won't know, since women in Russia tend to feel shame and fear for their lives if they report their abusers.

The message: Women aren't people.

Freedom to protest

In a story that gained international attention in 2012, the protest punk group "Pussy Riot" recorded part of a music video in a church that involved lip-syncing a song for 40 seconds. Three members, Maria Alyokhina, Yekaterina Samutsevich and Nadezhda Tolokonnikova, were tried for "hooliganism motivated by religious hatred" and found guilty. Alyokhina and Tolokonnikova, both mothers in their early twenties at the time, were sentenced to secret labor camps.

The message: Opinions are meant to be kept inside a tomb and never from someone with a womb.

Freedom to be gay

In 2013, President Putin signed a bill into law that would prohibit "propaganda of nontraditional sexual relations to minors." Basically, he's telling Russians not to publicly be gay.

The message: Straight, white men are superior.

Bonus Tip:

How to get over the wall: use a ladder.

Chapter 10: Resist

We were brought here as religious refugees from the Soviet Union to escape blind oppression and to be given the chance to live freely, give freely, and think freely. We didn't sign up for this shit. The first nine chapters will help you survive this outrageous and unpredictable time, and this chapter will help you resist it. Attempt at your own peril.

Host a Putin Potluck

Mobilize your friends and neighbors for a resistance potluck. Instead of just gathering and bringing the usual dishes like mac-n-cheese, experiment with new recipes like borscht, eggplant ragu, piroshki (the Russian empanada) and vareniki (the Russian dumpling). Russian food is actually very tasty. Also, once you've all gathered to discuss how to mobilize the next march or sing-in, you'll actually appear to be one of "them" — you know, in case "they" stop by.

How to Make A Difference

Jury Duty: after years of deferring and having more kids to gain extended deferment, it's finally time to serve the people! Jury Duty is a great time to catch up on your junk mail or clean out your inbox, dust off your sketchbook and do some quick studies of people asleep and drooling. It's also a chance to weigh in on a potentially interesting and unique case. Plus: if you're lucky you may get quarantined like OJ's jury and then you'll make some lifelong friends. It's the closest thing to prison except with take-out and you even get to wear your own clothes.

Talk to people who don't agree with you: you're already an expert at this. Turn your skills from the annual Thanksgiving dinner fight into a tactical and practical skill. Before you embark on this practice your yoga breathing. You've got to stay calm to carry on to make a difference.

Get to know the local cops: what better time to hone your baking skills than now? Get your kids to help you with this. They should learn at a young age that police officers can be bribed with snacks.

Get to know your neighbors. There are many advantages to this. This is both a friendly gesture, but also a survival tactic. Start out with safe topics, and hopefully they'll be the ones to break the ice on joining the resistance. And, then you can bond and feel grateful that your neighbor is keeping an eye on you. Or, are you keeping an eye on them?

Volunteer! How can you not volunteer? Every politician, campaign, and shelter is desperate for your help. Just update your Facebook status to: Ready to volunteer! And you'll be riddled with suggestions and calls to action.

How to find local town halls

The easiest way is to visit www.townhallproject.com. The Russian way is to ask your cousin for the tip-off because they are helping out in keeping a close eye on the ones speaking out. Either way, you should go in disguise.

How to find a cause

Want to join the resistance but don't know how to choose? Talk to friends who are already involved and figure out which cause will be the best match for your busy schedule and won't interfere with your SoulCycle classes (that you sneak into and don't pay for). Don't feel bad. You can't help a cause unless you're helping yourself.

How to work on that cause

Make sure you've met your weekly cardio and step goal. If not, find a cause that involves door to door canvassing.

Other things you can do:

Get involved with Action Group Network. They will help to mobilize and connect you with like-minded individuals and activists groups near you, or just help you find local events and ways to be part of the resistance in your hometown:
http://actiongroups.net
Galvanize highlights organizations that need your time and money, important political issues and races, individuals who inspire us and the most significant news stories of the moment.
https://tinyletter.com/Galvanize
Make calls and keep up to date on congressional bills. This is a great resource:
www.indivisibleguide.com.

Run for local office.

Use your skills and talents to be heard. If you you're a writer, help organizations write newsletters. If you're a performer, donate your services once in a while to fundraisers.

If you have no skills, you can still help. Learn about town halls in your area, and share the information with at least five people in your neighborhood.

Volunteer or work on campaigns. Designate a day or a weekend once or twice a year to help on local, mayoral, gubernatorial, congressional, senatorial, or Presidential elections. Make calls, hand out flyers, let marginalized people know they're not alone.

Resist.

Bonus Tip

Run for office. Yeah, you (girl).

THE AUTHORS

Isabella & Vicky are two Soviet-born religious refugees who have navigated two identities and cultures for their entire lives. They met in ballet class when they were five and became instant best friends and creative collaborators. For close to three decades they have been using their humor and observational skills and gathering the exact information needed for a book like this…without even knowing it. Isabella is an interior designer with two kids, an American husband, a cat, and a Russian family who won't leave her alone. Vicky is a stand-up comedian and author of the comedic novel *The Russian Drop*. She was voted best stand-up at the United Solo Festival and has recorded two stand-up comedy albums. Isabella and Vicky's first collaboration was when they were ten and hosted their own radio show "Interview with Gorbachev," recorded in Vicky's kitchen in Brookline, Massachusetts.

FOLLOW US ON SOCIAL

Facebook	@HowToSpyOnYourNeighbor
Twitter	@HowToSpy
Instagram	@howtospyonyourneighbor

www.ingramcontent.com/pod-product-compliance
Lightning Source LLC
LaVergne TN
LVHW041223080426
835508LV00011B/1063